THE 4 PRINCIPLES OF
Dominion
Authority

Your Authority & Power to Create Success in Your Life!

HENRY L. RAZOR

S.H.E. PUBLISHING, LLC

The 4 Principles of Dominion Authority
Copyright © 2021 by Henry L. Razor.

All rights reserved. Printed in the United States of America. No part of this booklet may be used or reproduced in any manner whatsoever without written permission except in the case of brief quotations embodied in critical articles or reviews.

For information contact :
www.shepublishingllc.com
info@shepublishingllc.com

Book Cover design by Michelle Hudson

ISBN: 978-1-953163-31-8

Revised Edition : December 2021

10 9 8 7 6 5 4 3 2 1

DEDICATION

This booklet is dedicated to one of the GREATEST churches in the world! Faith Hope & Charity Ministries in Chicago, Illinois; Otherwise known as The Faith Place-Chicago!

CONTENTS

INTRODUCTION i

You Are a Living Soul 1

Desire It 7

Speak It 11

Believe It 15

Act Upon It 18

The Power of the Holy Spirit 21

ACKNOWLEDGEMENTS

First, I give thanks to God for His direction and guidance while preparing this work for distribution.

To my wife, Janette, who was very patient with me during this project, I say, 'Honey, I thank you so much.

To the leadership team at The Faith Place-Chicago, you guys are one in a million, and your commitment to the success of this ministry and perfection is unmatched.

I must acknowledge Michelle Hudson for the brilliant cover design and to the entire Faith Hope & Charity Church family, many of you have for years requested of me to write. I thank God for such a loving church.

Pastor Henry L. Razor

and have dominion over the fish of the sea, and over the fowl of the air, and over every living thing that moveth upon the earth.

Genesis 1:28 KJV

INTRODUCTION

The law of man's Living Soul Dominion Authority is one of the least preached laws of God in sermons, one of the least taught laws of God in lessons, and one of the least emphasized biblical laws in our church today. Yet, when appropriately understood and implemented as God purposed it, this law is undoubtedly the most powerful law to impact change at every level of existence.

Note: I will interchangeably use the terms' Dominion Authority' and 'Living Soul Dominion Authority' throughout this booklet. After reading the first chapter of this booklet, it should be clear that they are one and the same.

Implementation of the law of Dominion Authority has the power to force change at the personal level in your life as things that the principles of this law are applied to <u>must</u> change in accordance with your usage of this law. It also has the power to force change at the community level in your life if implemented within the areas where you must engage the community. This law is so powerful that it impacts change at national, international, and global levels when those levels intersect with your desire.

Within leadership functions, three circles exist that connect and intersect with every human on the face of this earth. These circles are universally accepted and are utilized to explain the power and influence that everyone has. The law of Living Soul Dominion Authority impact within each of these three circles according to the application of the laws by you, as an individual.

[1]

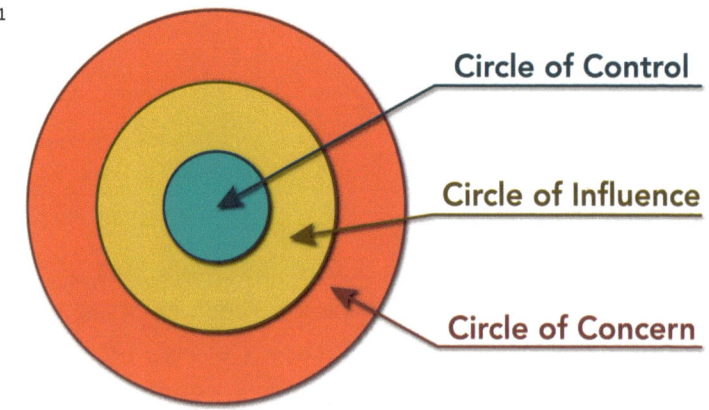

- **Circle of Control:** These things you have direct control over, such as your actions and your responses to adversity and opportunities.

---

[1] Dr. Stephen Covey's "The Seven Habits of Highly Effective People"

- **Circle of Influence:** These things you have indirect control over, such as other peoples' reactions, their thoughts. But, unlike the Circle of Concern, you can still influence action or change.

- **Circle of Concern:** These are areas that concern you but in which you generally have little or no control, such as national debt, weather or traffic.

Once you properly apply the laws of the Living Soul Dominion Authority to the situations in your life, your circle of concern will change, your influences will increase, and your area of control will be enlarged. You will experience powerful results that will forever change your life.

I was born in the impoverished Mississippi Delta, when the region suffered from immense poverty and lack. I grew up working in the fields, chopping cotton during the summer months and picking cotton during the fall. I was fortunate to come along when school was mandatory, so we had to attend, even though we needed to earn money from working the fields. I thank God for the teachers I had because they emphasized reading with comprehension as a foundation for creating a better life. Then in 1975, Missionary Ella Mae Banks asked permission of my mom to take me to the Earle Church of God in Christ with her. There I was introduced to the Bible, and my life forever changed.

The bible mentioned all of the things that I could have and could be. Many things appeared to be well out of my reach, but I could have them according to what I read in the bible. This is where I learned of Living Soul Dominion Authority. No one there ever taught me about my Dominion Authority; they said I should read the bible and apply the teachings. As I read, I understood that God had invested so much power in me as a person that none of the things that I desired were out of my reach. I had to go and get them.

Over time, I evolved from the Poverty of the Mississippi Delta to Global Technical Engineering Manager. I went from living in a four-room house with fourteen other siblings and sleeping in the 'boy's bed' with all of my brothers, to acquiring multiple real estate properties that continue to appreciate in value. This all occurred because I acquired the knowledge of the Dominion Authority that God gave me when he created me, then I utilized this authority to change my life and the general course of my life.

I will, in this booklet, introduce and explain, with biblical support, the four principles of the Living Soul Dominion Authority that everyone has. Then I will introduce the Holy Spirit, who provides even more power to impact change in this world.

It is my prayer that this booklet lights the fire that will create a burning success that you experience all the days of your life.

You Are a Living Soul

BEFORE I JUMP INTO THE FOUR PRINCIPLES of living Soul Dominion, I must first introduce and define the term 'Living Soul.' For this, I must briefly mention the constitution (*or the makeup*) of man.

We see that in Genesis, man consists of:[2]

- A body formed from the dust of the earth
- A soul from God that makes us in His image
- A spirit that quickened the body and gives life to the soul

For a detailed explanation of the constitution of man, I refer you to my previous book, **'Winning Spiritual Wars'**. In this book, you will find the constitution explained in simple language with biblical support and scriptural references.

Of the three elements of man listed above, only one element is material and physical in nature. That is the body. The soul and the spirit are not physical or material; hence they belong to the immaterial spiritual world. *Once again, this is explained in the Winning Spiritual Wars book.*

The interesting thing about the constitution of man is found in the first and second chapter of Genesis. God creates then re-organized a physical earth. He then creates physical creatures to inhabit this physical earth. He then creates a three-element man with two elements, spiritual and one element physical. He then refers to this man as a 'Living Soul'[3], not a living body! WOW! In the realm of the physical earth, God created man to exist as a soul, more specifically a **'Living Soul'**! But wait, the earth is material and physical, whereas the soul is immaterial and spiritual. But why would God place an immaterial spiritual soul within the realm of a material physical earth? In a word, **DOMINION**!

---

[2] Genesis 2:7; 1 Thessalonians 5:23

[3] Genesis 2:7

In my book, Winning Spiritual Wars, I explain that the spiritual world is the world of supernatural beings. Angels, for example, reside, and they are not natural beings. Our souls also reside in this world. This would mean that our souls are supernatural. I also point out in Winning Spiritual Wars that the limitations of the natural world do not constrain beings that reside in the supernatural world. This would mean that the limitations of the natural world do not constrain our supernatural soul. This makes it easy for the soul to exercise dominion and authority on the earth.

But the soul, being spiritual, can't impact the physical world unless it is allowed to. Without being allowed, the soul will take a back seat to the physical body in the realm of the physical earth. So regardless of how easy it is, the spiritual soul can't overrule the physical body on the physical earth. I go into detail on this in my book Winning Spiritual Wars.

Since man was given dominion and will take that dominion regardless, the key to implementation is the spirit. Remember that once the spirit was 'breathed' into man, the body came to life, but that's also when man became a Living Soul. So it was also when the soul became active or came alive, and the dominion of man commenced!

So, if a man's spirit has NOT been regenerated, Dominion Authority will be executed in an ungodly manner, whereas, if one has received the spirit of Christ and their spirit has been regenerated, they will execute Dominion Authority in accordance with the laws of God.

The key here is that Dominion Authority is a function of being a human or a Living Soul. All living people have this authority and will either implement it or yield it to others that execute it.

I must pause here and emphasize that God never intended men to exercise Dominion Authority over other men. Jesus said in Luke 22:25-26 KJV:

> 25. And he said unto them, the kings of the Gentiles exercise lordship over them; and they that exercise authority upon them are called benefactors.
>
> 26. But ye *shall* not be so: but he that is greatest among you, let him be as...

Living Souls were created to live in harmony with each other and dominion was to be exercised over the creatures and all other non-human beings within the realm of this earth. I refer here to another previous book penned by myself entitled 'Biblically Black and Blessed.' In this book, I explain the assignments that God has given to all men. I explain how the will of God is for every Living Soul to dwell on this earth in harmony.

Now, back to Dominion Authority...

Dominion Authority is a benefit of being human, and it will be implemented regardless of the state of the human. If the spirit has not been regenerated, this authority will be used in ways that do not align with God's will or His plan for humanity. When it is exercised as such, things like chattel slavery, unjust laws, oppression, sexism, racism, income inequality, etc., become prominent in society. Especially if those who are victims of such unjustness remain silent and neglect to take a stand, thereby neglecting the dominion they also possess, when those who are the victims of this unjustness take a stand, they exercise their dominion, and things change. They don't change overnight, but they change because God never intended for humans to exercise dominion over other humans.

One of the most significant examples of Dominion Authority being exercised to correct a wrong can be seen in the plight of African Americans in the United States. Men and women on the continent of Africa were forcibly brought to America and lorded over by men with un-regenerated spirits. These oppressive men were exercising dominion against the ways of God. But as the men and women who were the victims stood up, they began exercising their Dominion Authority, so things changed. It didn't change overnight, and change still needs to occur, but change commenced. People like Gabriel Prosser, Nat Turner, Martin Luther King, Malcolm X, Jesse Jackson, Harriet Tubman, Sojourner Truth, and others lead the way in the fight to correct the wrongs of society.

Note that I refer to the plight of African Americans in America in the context of African Americans exercising Dominion Authority.

Think about it.

African Americans were outnumbered in this country. The oppressor had the weapons, the resources, and the power. And the oppressor had no intentions of changing. Only Dominion Authority, as authorized by God, could create the change that we now experience. And when the oppressed stood up, they began exercising their Dominion Authority, and things had to change.

This, in a nutshell, is Dominion Authority at work.

It is this same Dominion Authority that God expects us to use in the correct way to impact positive change at every level of our lives. God created us to create success, generate wealth, and positively impact our families, communities, and the world. No good thing can be withheld from you[4] if you use this authority as God purposed for it.

The Bible lays out the principles for using this authority, and in the following pages of this booklet, I will cover each of these principles.

---

[4] Psalms 84:11

Desire It

PRINCIPLE 1

DESIRE - a strong feeling of wanting to have something or wishing for something to happen.

This would be the first principle needed to implement Dominion Authority and create change for obvious reasons. To accomplish anything, you must desire to accomplish it, or there's no need to start on it. Note that desire is defined as a **strong** feeling of wanting something to happen. The road to acquisition and accomplishment must always begin with desire.

If you are sick, you must want to be well for wellness to come. If you are financially challenged, you must want to acquire wealth before the resources manifest. If you are lonely, you must want to have a relationship before crossing roads with a connection. If you are sad, you must want to be happy before the joy arrives. Yes, the road to successful acquisition always begins with desire. Proverbs 10:24 KJV reads:

> *The fear of the wicked, it shall come upon him: but the desire of the righteous shall be granted.*

It is worthy of note that the desire of the righteous shall be granted. Earlier I mentioned that the spirit is key in determining whether Dominion will be exercised as God intended for it to be exercised or exercised in an unGodly manner. I also emphasized that because man has been granted Dominion, this Dominion will be exercised whether the man is Godly or not. But this afore referenced scripture would explain how Dominion Authority led to freedom for slaves and rights for those that were mistreated. When those unjustly treated desired freedom, equality, fairness, and just treatment, they stood and spoke up for those things. Those that were in power were exercising Dominion in an unGodly manner, and when the victims stood up, God stood up for them. God granted the desires because they were righteous desires. Whenever the Godly exercising of Dominion opposes unGodly exercising of Dominion, God stands for the Godly, and their desire is granted. Even when people are powerless within the system, exercising Dominion in a Godly manner brings God to their aid and results in phenomenal accomplishment. Psalms 10:17 KJV reads:

> *LORD, thou hast heard the desire of the humble: thou wilt prepare their heart, thou wilt cause thine ear to hear:*

God has tied Himself to the humble and righteous with such a bond that their desires are ever before Him, and He will grant these desires as a Parent does an obedient child. Psalms 38:9 KJV reads:

> Lord, all my **desire** is before thee;
> and my groaning is not hidden from thee.

He will grant these desires because the righteous always strive to do what's pleasing to Him. Psalms 37:4 KJV reads:

> Delight thyself also in the LORD,
> and he shall give thee the desires of thine heart.

Desire is vital in successfully exercising your Dominion Authority because earnest desire will force you to accomplish your goal or acquire the things desired. We know that faith without works is dead[5]. So the action produced by your desire demonstrates to God that you are expecting to accomplish your goal and receive what you desire. I like the biblical book of James because it is practical teaching for successful living. James even goes on to say that he can show you his earnest desires (faith) by letting you observe whether or not he has taken action to accomplish or acquire the thing desired. James 2:18 KJV reads:

> Yea, a man may say, Thou hast faith, and I have works:
> shew me thy faith without thy works,
> and I will shew thee my faith by my works.

So you must add to your earnest desire the works that show that you expect to accomplish what you desire or that you expect to

---

[5] James 2:14-26

receive what you request.

We are instructed to inform God of our desires through prayer, so this must be the initiator for the realization of our desires. Simply put, we start by speaking our desires in prayer. I will talk later on about the importance of what we say in exercising Dominion authority. But at this point, I want to emphasize the importance of prayer with faith to obtain what we desire. Mark 11:24 KJV reads:

*Therefore, I say unto you, What things soever ye **desire**, when ye pray, believe that ye receive them, and ye shall have them.*

Here Jesus teaches us that when we speak our desires in prayer and believe that those desires will be granted, God will grant them.

So in order to experience success when implementing your Dominion Authority, you must possess the earnest desire for a thing and take action while believing that your action will produce the desired results!

However, this is only the first principle for exercising your Dominion Authority, but it is foundational.

Speak It

PRINCIPLE 2

Sometimes I believe that we as humans don't realize how powerful our words are. The Dominion Authority that God has given us first comes to life through our words.

We were created in Gods' image and likeness[6]. Just as God accomplishes His will in the earth by speaking, our words are also used to accomplish what we want or to exercise Dominion Authority. We see man's likeness to God in this area in the first

---

[6] Genesis 1:26-27

two chapters of Genesis. In the first chapter, God speaks, and the world is reorganized at the sound of His voice. Then in chapter two, Adam speaks, and all the creatures that God created received identification at the voice of Adam. Adam was the authority figure on the earth, just as God was the authority figure throughout the universe.

What you say is an essential principle of Dominion Authority.
Mark 11:23 KJV reads:

> *For verily I say unto you, That whosoever shall say unto this mountain, Be thou removed, and be thou cast into the sea; and shall not doubt in his heart, but shall believe that those things which he saith shall come to pass;*
> *he shall have whatsoever he saith.*

Look at this! You can have whatsoever you say, so long as you say it without doubting that it will happen. So your Dominion Authority will become successful as long as you speak it with confidence and authority, never doubting that you will be successful in your endeavor. Throughout Genesis chapter 1, when God said, "Let there be," it was. And throughout Genesis chapter two, whatever Adam called each creature is what they became; plain and simple Dominion!

The Words That You Speak Are Powerful!
Proverbs 18:21 KJV reads:

> *Death and life are in the power of the tongue:*

Herein is the power within this principle for exercising your Dominion Authority. If you say it, you will see it. What you say it will be is exactly what it will be. Stop saying how bad things are because as long as you speak it, it will be so. Start saying how good God is and verbally calling for good and positive things to occur in your life. When you do this, you will experience positive results.

I'm reminded of a question that God once asked Jeremiah.
Jeremiah 1:11-12 reads:

> 11. *Moreover the word of the LORD came unto me, saying, Jeremiah, what seest thou? And I said, I see a rod of an almond tree.*
>
> 12. *Then said the LORD unto me, Thou hast well seen: for I will hasten my word to perform it.*

God asks Jeremiah what does he see? Jeremiah responds, and God says, you have seen well. I will quickly cause this to happen. I know that in this verse, Jeremiah was seeing the discipline of God upon a disobedient people. But God allowed Jeremiah to determine by his words, the form of discipline would be applied. What I find interesting here is that God didn't show Jeremiah something and explain to him what He was showing. He instructs Jeremiah to look and tell Him what he is seeing. What do you see in your situation? When exercising Dominion Authority, you must look through the eyes of faith and see the best possible solution, the solution that you earnestly desire. Then you must verbally proclaim that this outcome is what you see. And because it is what you desire and what you speak, it is what will happen. Your results will match what you proclaim because of your Dominion Authority when you begin to do this.

Have you ever wondered what would have happened if Jeremiah had responded that he saw a less severe form of discipline being applied to bring the rebellious people back into obedience? Since God responded to Jeremiah's answer by saying, "you saw well, I will quickly do what you saw," would God have also quickly done a less severe discipline if that was what Jeremiah had spoken? Oh, the power of what you say!

Remember that God created us in His image and after His likeness; therefore, we ought to do things the way that He does things. And God speaks things into existence and calls things that are not as though they are. Romans 4:16-17 KJV reads:

16. *Therefore it is of faith, that it might be by grace; to the end the promise might be sure to all the seed; not to that only which is of the law, but to that also which is of the faith of Abraham; who is the father of us all,*

17. *(As it is written, I have made thee a father of many nations,) before him whom he believed, even God, who quickeneth the dead, and calleth those things which be not as though they were.*

Believe It

PRINCIPLE 3

I never realized that our Dominion Authority also depends heavily on our ability to believe in the authority. If God gave us this authority, then it's obvious that it will work the way He purposed it and accomplish what you want to accomplish. But Dominion Authority is exercised in the face of opposition. Just because you have the authority to perform an action doesn't mean that all of your opposition is going to back away, lay down, and permit you to use your authority without fighting back. But it's when comfronted with this opposition that you must remember that you are the Person of Authority in any conflict with the enemy; as the Person of Authority, you need not fight, only speak your desire and have faith. Your God will do the rest!

Recall how Michael the Archangel faced opposition, and you must confront your opposition the same way. "SPEAK YOUR DESIRE AND BELIEVE"! Jude verse 9 KJV reads:

"Yet Michael the archangel, when contending with the devil he disputed about the body of Moses, durst not bring against him a railing accusation, but said, The Lord rebuke thee."

Faith has been, is currently, and will always be the cornerstone of anything and everything that we do under God's directive. So the Dominion that God has given us must be exercised through faith! Hebrews 11:6 KJV reads:

*But without faith, **it is** impossible to please **him**:*

So this principle of Dominion Authority simply insists that you believe what you speak. Look at the links that we have connected thus far:

> You must **Believe** what You **Speak**
> You must **Speak** what You **Desire**
> You Begin with a **Desire**

This is awesome, but as of yet, it is not complete. We will add the fourth principle a little later in this booklet.

This reminds me of a story that I heard a preacher tell many years ago. This is how it goes:

There was a man that owned a house in the valley. There were mountains very close to his house, both on the east side of him and on the west side of him. So basically, he lived in darkness. In the mornings, when the sun arose, the mountains cast a shadow over his house, so it was dark. During the evening sunset, they also cast a shadow over his house from the other direction. Then at midday, when the sun was directly over him, the roof of his house blocked it, so he remained in darkness. But once he read in the bible that he could speak to the mountain and tell them to be removed, they would have to obey. He was skeptical but willing to try anything to get a little sunlight. So one day, he got on his knees and prayed that the mountain on the west be removed so he could get a little sunlight during the evenings. He got up off of his knees after praying and saw that nothing has happened. The mountain is still there. When he saw this, he said, "just like I thought, this doesn't work at all." If you don't expect that what you speak will come to pass, there is no need to speak it. You must speak with confidence and know that **faith always produces the desired results!**

In 1 Kings chapter 17, Elijah confidently informs Ahab that there will be no more rain until he says so. This is the confidence that we must speak our desire when exercising our Dominion Authority! 1 Kings 17:1 KJV reads:

And Elijah the Tishbite, who was of the inhabitants of Gilead, said unto Ahab, As the LORD God of Israel liveth, before whom I stand, there shall not be dew nor rain these years, but according to my word.

Elijah makes it plain that he is exercising the Dominion Authority that God has given him. He didn't doubt or waver but spoke his desire with confidence. He emphasized this by saying I am speaking this to you by the authority granted to me by God, before whom I currently stand. By wording his statement this way, it's as if Elijah is saying, "I'm making this statement by the authority of God, and if you don't believe I have this authority, God's right here standing with me, ask Him!"

THAT'S CONFIDENCE!

It is with this faith that we must exercise our Dominion Authority!

Act Upon It

PRINCIPLE 4

This fourth principle is the area where I have observed the most trepidation among believers. Many Believers are reluctant to act on what they believe without a physical, tangible indicator of progress or success. But that's not how Dominion Authority works. In actuality, that's not even how faith works. Remember, as previously stated, that faith without works is dead. So it is this principle that completes the cycle of bringing what you desire into reality.

> You Must **Take Action On** What You **Believe**
> You Must **Believe** What You **Speak**
> You Must **Speak** What You **Desire**
> You Begin with a **Desire**

Your actions are the primary indicator of your belief in what you have spoken. Remember James said if you show him a person who has faith without works, he'll show you his faith by his works.

So, James says you can see the actions that he's taking and know that he has faith. This verse is worth revisiting: James 2:18 KJV reads:

Yea, a man may say,
Thou hast faith, and I have works:
shew me thy faith without thy works,
and I will shew thee my faith by my works.

So how is it that my actions are a display of my faith? When exercising Dominion Authority, you must take actions on what you desire and believe, not on the situation as it currently is. This is what transforms what you believe into what **actually is**.

Simply put, you can't pray, say that you believe, but do nothing, and expect to get something. Hebrews 11:1 tells us that faith is the substance of things **hoped** for. Then Romans 8:24 KJV tells us that hope that is seen is not hope.

So by taking action on what I believe through faith, I am acting on what I cannot currently see, but my actions will cause it to come forth, materialize, and it will be seen.

I never understood those in the church who just prayed and expected God to do things God has given them the authority to do. Your prayer must always be accompanied by actions that demonstrate that you believe that what you are praying for will happen.

You can't just pray and expect God to make your business successful. After you pray, you need to create a marketing plan, market your product or service, analyze trends relative to your product or service, collect metrics and adjust your business plan accordingly. God said to Joshua that he had the power to make his way prosperous, and he had this same authority to create success. Joshua 1:8 KJV reads:

For then thou shalt make thy way prosperous,

and then thou shalt have success.

Two points stand out in God's directive to Joshua.

1. Joshua has to have a **way** to experience prosperity and success. Your way is your plan for accomplishing what you desire. It's your business. It's your idea. It's your invention. It's the work that you select to bring you to the place of success that you desire. Without a way, you have nothing to make prosperous and nothing to make successful.

2. You are the one responsible for making your way prosperous and creating success. God did not say that He would do this; He said that you must do this. But you can only do this by first following His commandments, guidelines, and ways for humanity. This goes back to starting the Dominion Authority process with the **'right desire'**.

Have you taken the time to consider what your 'way' is? Did you start the process of making your way prosperous and creating success with the **'right desire'**?

Simply put, this principle indicates whether or not you even believe that you have Dominion Authority. It is more than just wanting, or just speaking, or just saying you believe. Exercising Dominion Authority is a process that starts with your desire and ends with that desire being realized. But you must apply all of the principles to achieve success!

The Power of the Holy Spirit

I conclude this booklet by briefly summarizing the function of the Holy Spirit in exercising Living Soul Dominion Authority. It is said that if I have this much Power and Authority, what do I need the Holy Spirit for? We must consider the biblically stated purpose of the Holy Spirit, and then we can see the role it plays in Dominion Authority and in the earth in general.

The Apostles were notified that they would get power when they received the Holy Spirit. Acts 1:8 KJV reads:

> *But ye shall receive power,*
> *after that the Holy Ghost comes upon you:*

But this same verse informs them what they would be empowered to do when they received it.

> *And ye shall be witnesses unto me both in Jerusalem,*
> *And in all Judæa, and Samaria,*
> *And unto the uttermost part of the earth.*

So the power of the Holy Spirit would empower them to be witnesses, or empower them to carry out God's will on the earth. And this is the power we receive as a result of receiving the spirit of Christ in our lives. We are empowered to carry out God's will on the earth. When we do this, the prayer that Jesus taught us to pray is answered. Matthew 6:10 KJV reads:

> *Thy kingdom come.*
> *Thy will be done in earth, as it is in heaven.*

The Holy Ghost is the manifestation of God in the earth so that He may work His will in the earth through us. This is how His kingdom comes! The Holy Spirit empowers us to establish the Kingdom of God on the earth. Romans 14:17 KJV reads:

> *For the kingdom of God is not meat and drink, but*
> *righteousness, and peace, and joy in the Holy Ghost.*

So the primary function and purpose of the Holy Ghost (Spirit) is to empower us to bring the 'Kingdom of God' to men while on the earth. In so doing, it is a comforter, a guide, a recaller of things to our memory, etc. All of these functions work to establish the Kingdom of God on the earth. Jesus said in Luke 17:20-21 KJV:

> *The kingdom of God cometh not with observation:*
> *Neither shall they say, Lo here! or, lo there! for, behold, <u>the</u>*
> <u>*kingdom of God is within you.*</u>

But there is another function of the Holy Spirit that is more intrinsically tied to the use of our Dominion Authority. Since the process of operating in Dominion Authority begins with the right desire, the Holy Spirit ensures that our desires are aligned with the will of God. And since the very first principle of Dominion Authority is Desire it, Holy Spirit ensures that you begin exercising your authority in alignment with God's will.

This goes back to the spiritual regeneration that occurs when Holy Spirit enters. And since Genesis indicated that the spirit quickened the body and initiated the Living Soul, a regenerated spirit would also ensure that your desires align with the will of God. This is a very brief synopsis of this subject. For a more detailed explanation, I recommend that you obtain a copy of **Winning Spiritual Wars**. Holy Spirit's relationship with Body and Soul is explained in detail there.

I pray that this booklet blesses you and motivates you to use all of the Authority that God has invested in you.

I decree health, wealth, prosperity, and much success as you implement the principles of this book.

Pastor Henry L Razor

www.ingramcontent.com/pod-product-compliance
Lightning Source LLC
Chambersburg PA
CBHW041215070526
44579CB00001B/5